ANIMALS
ANIMALS

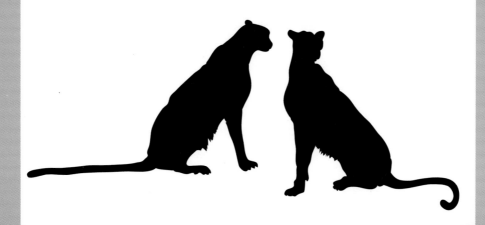

CHEETAHS

BY DIANA ESTIGARRIBIA

BENCHMARK BOOKS

MARSHALL CAVENDISH
NEW YORK

Series Consultant
James Doherty
General Curator
Bronx Zoo, New York

Benchmark Books
Marshall Cavendish
99 White Plains Road
Tarrytown, NY 10591–9001
www.marshallcavendish.com

Library of Congress Cataloging–in–Publication Data

Estigarribia, Diana.
Cheetahs / by Diana Estigarribia.
p. cm. – (Animals, animals)
Summary: Describes the physical characteristics, behavior, hunting methods, and habitat of cheetahs.
Includes bibliographical references (p.   ) and index.
ISBN 0–7614–1749–4
1. Cheetah–Juvenile literature. [1. Cheetah.] I. Title. II. Series.

QL737.C23E78 2004
599.75'9–dc22
2003022600

Photo Research by Joan Meisel

Cover photo: Paul A. Souders/Corbis

Photographs in this book are used by permission and through the courtesy of: *Corbis*: W. Perry Conway, 4; Stapleton collection, 8; Martin Harvey, 10, 39; Gallo Images: Theo Allofs, 14–15; Tom Brakefield, 16; Winifred Wisniewski, 23; Frank Lane Picture Agency: Paul A. Souders, 26, 36; Galen Rowell, 28; Torleif Svensson, 30–31. *Peter Arnold, Inc.*: Yann Arthus-Bertrand, 6; Martin Harvey 18, 21; Denis-Huot, 24–25; Gerard Lacz, 33; Fritz Polking 34, 40.

Printed in China
1 3 5 6 4 2

CONTENTS

1
INTRODUCING CHEETAHS

The cheetah is Earth's fastest land mammal. Cheetahs can reach top speeds of about 70 miles per hour (112 km/hr), covering 20 feet (7 meters) with each stride. The cheetah's speed is so great that it appears to fly through the air. Between strides a cheetah's feet come off the ground. Cheetahs need large open lands for chasing prey at such high speed.

Cheetahs live in savannas, which are open grasslands, and in woodlands. They live in small groups—either a small group of males or a single female and her cubs. Females and their offspring generally have larger territories than males, sometimes roaming over as much as 500 square miles (804 sq km) of land. Males generally keep to areas of around 40 square miles (65 sq km). Cheetahs live in the wild mainly in Namibia and Botswana in southern Africa, and Kenya and Tanzania in eastern Africa.

Since ancient times, cheetahs have been admired above all other cats for their speed and beautiful spotted coats.

A CHEETAH RESTS IN THE GRASS.

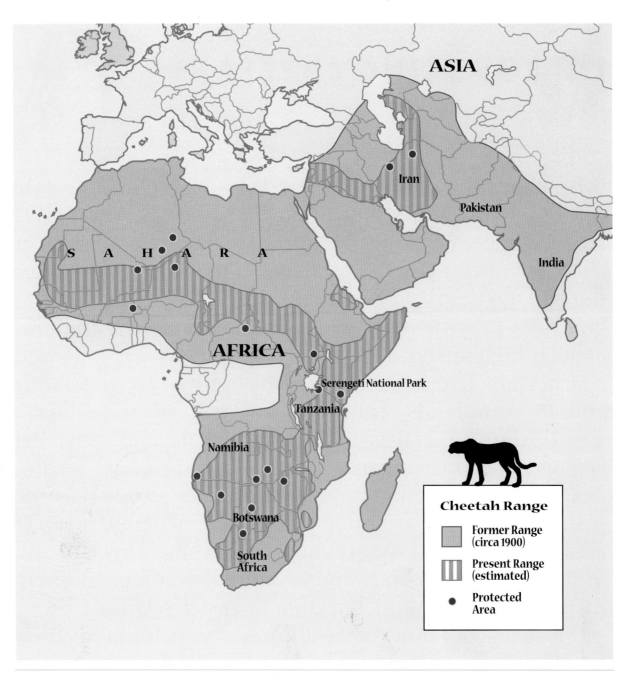

ASIA

Iran

Pakistan

India

S A H A R A

AFRICA

Serengeti National Park

Tanzania

Namibia

Botswana

South
Africa

Cheetah Range

Former Range
(circa 1900)

Present Range
(estimated)

Protected
Area

THIS MAP SHOWS WHERE CHEETAHS USED TO LIVE AND WHERE THEY LIVE
TODAY. THE BLACK DOTS INDICATE NATIONAL PARKS AND RESERVES.

CHEETAHS ARE OFTEN SEEN IN OPEN COUNTRY, BUT THEY ALSO LIVE IN DENSE WOODLANDS AND MOUNTAINOUS AREAS.

The cheetah's name comes from a Hindi word, chita, meaning spotted one. About 2,500 years ago the cheetah was kept as a trained hunter and a companion to emperors. The Egyptian pharaohs regarded the cheetah as a royal cat goddess that guarded the afterlife. In parts of the Middle East and in Egypt, the cheetah was known as the hunting leopard. The Mesopotamians, Minoans, and Egyptians captured and trained cheetahs to help human hunters pursue their game. Akbar the Great of India had over 3,000 cheetahs, and explorer Marco Polo observed that Kublai Khan kept hundreds of cheetahs as trained hunters.

PEOPLE THROUGHOUT EUROPE AND ASIA ONCE CAPTURED CHEETAHS TO HELP THEM HUNT.

In the ancient world, adult wild cheetahs were trapped, tamed, and trained to be hunting companions for people. Hunting game animals with the help of other animals is called *coursing*. A cheetah was kept on a leash, its head covered with a hood so it could not see its prey. Once a herd was spotted, the hunters would remove the hood and release the cheetah. The cheetah was rewarded with a treat of meat for each successful kill.

Cheetahs have been on Earth for millions of years. But the wild cheetah population has steadily disappeared from places where it once lived in abundant numbers, including Africa, Asia, and the Middle East. The Asian cheetah is extinct in India and Israel, and possibly only two to three hundred remain in Iran. Several factors have cut the number of Namibian cheetahs in half to only about 2,500 animals. The more people learn about these swift and beautiful predators, the better they can help them to survive in the future.

2
BUILT FOR SPEED

The cheetah is an unusual member of the cat family, which includes large meat-eating predators like lions, tigers, jaguars, and lynxes, as well as small *domestic* cats.

Unlike other cats of its size, the cheetah's slender body is built for speed instead of strength. An average cheetah weighs between 80 and 140 pounds (35–65 kilograms). With its deep, narrow chest, small head, and long, thin legs with doglike feet, the cheetah resembles a greyhound. From head to tail an adult cheetah measures about 7 feet (1-2 m), with a body length of $3\frac{1}{2}$ to $4\frac{1}{2}$ feet (1 to 1.4 m) and a 2- to 3-foot-long tail. Compared to most large cats, the cheetah is small and light.

The cheetah's tawny brown, spotted coat is short and coarse. The fur on its belly is white. The cheetah's tail has four to six rings toward the end with a bushy white tuft at the tip.

CHEETAHS CAN GO FROM A CROUCHING POSITION TO A SPRINTING SPEED OF 45 MILES (72 KM) PER HOUR WITHIN SECONDS.

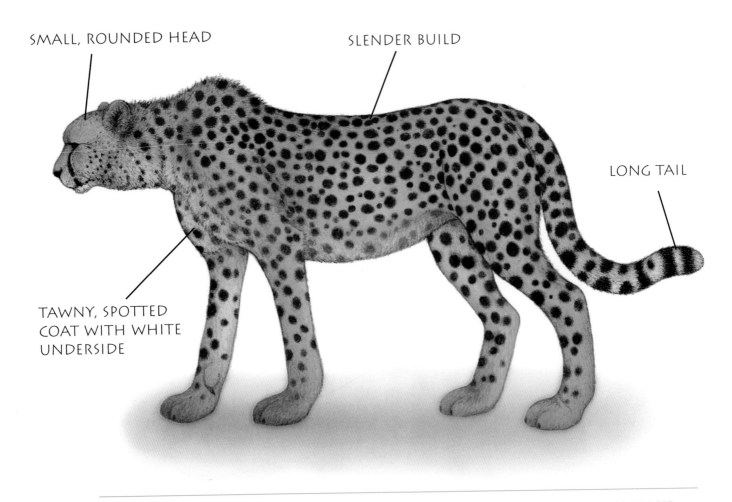

SMALL, ROUNDED HEAD

SLENDER BUILD

LONG TAIL

TAWNY, SPOTTED
COAT WITH WHITE
UNDERSIDE

THE CHEETAH'S SLENDER BUILD AND SMALL HEAD ARE TWO FEATURES THAT
ARE QUITE DIFFERENT FROM OTHER LARGE CATS.

One way to recognize a cheetah is by the black lines on
its face that resemble tear stains. These black markings
help the cheetah to see in the bright glare of the sun, and
help to hide the cheetah in tall grass.

Every part of the cheetah's unique body is built for

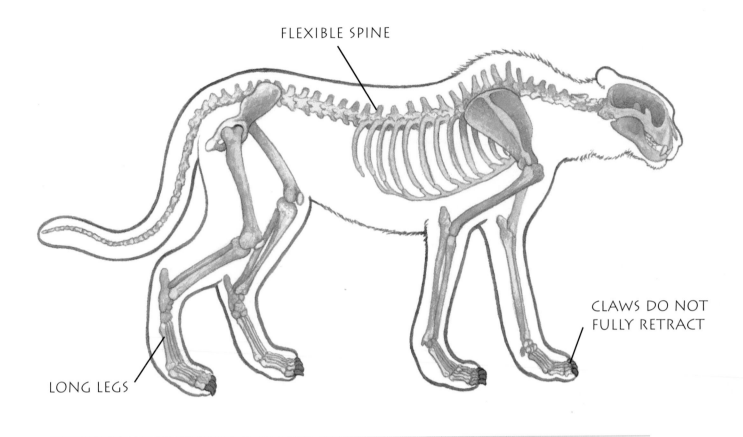

FLEXIBLE SPINE

CLAWS DO NOT
FULLY RETRACT

LONG LEGS

THE CHEETAH'S LONG LIMBS AND FLEXIBLE SPINE HELP IT TO COVER GREAT DISTANCES QUICKLY.

sprinting. The cheetah's long legs and feet and strong, flexible spine give it greater speed. The cheetah has strong, curved claws that grip the ground as it runs. This keeps the cat from slipping while it's running and turning. The toes can spread wide for greater traction. The cheetah's long, muscular tail helps it to balance.

13

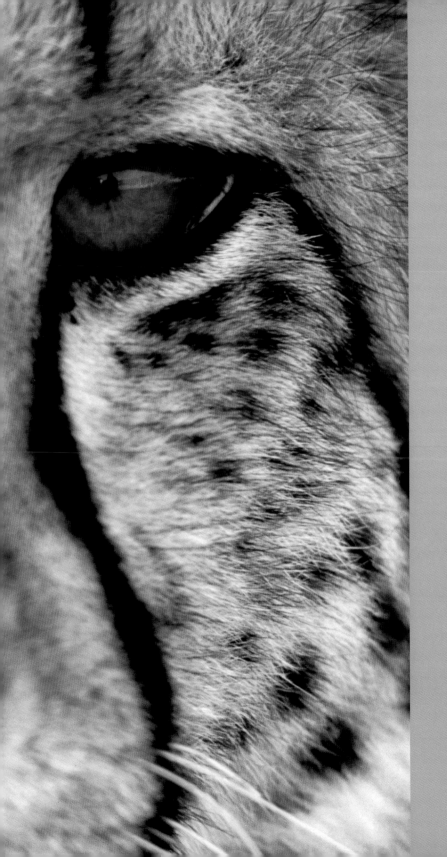

WHY THE CHEETAH'S CHEEKS ARE STAINED

ACCORDING TO A TRADITIONAL ZULU STORY, THE CHEETAH'S DISTINCTIVE TEAR STAINS APPEARED WHEN A SELFISH HUNTER STOLE A MOTHER CHEETAH'S CUBS. WHEN THE PEOPLE IN A NEARBY VILLAGE DISCOVERED WHAT THE HUNTER HAD DONE, THEY BANISHED THE HUNTER AND BEGAN TO SEARCH FOR THE CUBS. SOON AFTER, THE BABIES WERE SAFELY RETURNED. BUT THE MOTHER CHEETAH HAD CRIED SO MUCH FOR HER MISSING CUBS THAT HER TEARS MADE PERMANENT DARK STAINS DOWN HER CHEEKS.

AS A CHEETAH SPEEDS UP, ITS FLEXIBLE SPINE STRETCHES. CHEETAHS CAN COVER UP TO 20 FEET (7-8 M) WITH EACH STRIDE.

Large nostrils and sinuses allow more oxygen into the cheetah's lungs during a run. The cheetah relies on its powerful heart and large, strong arteries to make use of all this oxygen. But it can run for only short periods of time before it must rest. An average chase lasts around thirty seconds. In that time, a cheetah can cover 400 to 600 yards (364–546 m).

Cheetahs cannot growl or roar like other big cats do. Instead, the cheetah chirps, yelps, and churrs. Churring is a soft sound that can be heard up to 100 feet (30 m) away. Cheetahs also purr when they are happy. Mother cheetahs purr loudly when they are with their cubs.

3
A CHEETAH'S LIFE

When a female cheetah is about two years old, she is ready to mate and become a mother. A cheetah can breed in any season of the year and females breed about once every eighteen months. To let males know that she is ready to mate, a female will signal male cheetahs by scent marking–spraying urine on rocks, trees, or shrubs. Males sniff trees and rocks, checking their territory for evidence of other cheetahs. When one finds a female's scent mark he follows her trail, carefully approaching her. A female might also chirp to attract male cheetahs to her. Male cheetahs will fight each other for one female.

When she is ready to give birth, a female will find a *den*, a place where she can hide and protect her newborn

CHEETAH CUBS HAVE GRAYISH FUR CALLED A MANTLE THAT HELPS TO HIDE THEM FROM PREDATORS.

from predators. After about ninety days, she will give birth to a *litter* of as many as eight cubs. The tiny cubs are born blind, and will not be able to see until their eyes open about ten days after birth. They do not yet resemble adult cheetahs, as they are born with a dark gray coat that makes their spots almost invisible. This 3-inch-long (7.6 cm) gray fur is called the *mantle*. Some experts believe the mantle helps to *camouflage*, or hide, young cubs from predators. By the time the cubs are three months old, the mantle has fallen out and their familiar spotted tawny coat has grown in.

A cheetah mother and her cubs are constantly on the move. As soon as three weeks after birth the cubs begin to walk. About a month later they can leave the den, following their mother. But they are not yet mature enough to accompany the mother when she goes out to find food.

Cubs are left alone and unprotected when their mother goes to hunt. The cubs wait quietly, scarcely moving at all, listening, and watching for any danger. There are many threats to a young cub's life. A high number of cheetah cubs do not grow to adulthood. Hyenas feed on cheetah cubs, and lions will kill young cheetahs for sport.

CHEETAH CUBS OPEN THEIR EYES AT ABOUT TWO WEEKS.

Cubs may also die from natural disaster, such as a flood, and the mother will sometimes abandon weaker cubs.

Cubs can eat meat when they are two months old. The mother will bring the kill to her litter, tearing and pulling the skin back for her cubs because cubs' teeth are still not strong enough to cut meat. While they eat, she stands back and watches for predators.

As the cubs grow, they start to imitate their mother and practice hunting with one another. One cub becomes the prey while brothers or sisters are the hunters. The mother may capture a small gazelle or fawn and release it for her cubs to chase. By playing these hunting games, young cubs learn the valuable skills they will need as adult cheetahs. By the age of ten months, cubs can catch small prey like gazelles, fawns, or warthog piglets. When they are about eighteen months old, they can hunt on their own.

When the cubs are grown, the males and females separate. A young female will go and find her own territory. She may live near other related females. She roams her territory alone. Female cheetahs do not live in groups as lionesses do.

CHEETAH OFFSPRING STAY WITH THEIR MOTHER UNTIL THEY ARE ABOUT
TWO YEARS OLD.

WHEN THEY ARE SIX MONTHS
OLD, YOUNG CHEETAHS MAY START
PRACTICING THEIR HUNTING
SKILLS ON LIVE PREY.

BROTHERS FROM THE SAME LITTER OR UNRELATED MALES MAY FORM A
COALITION THAT STAYS TOGETHER FOR LIFE.

Male cheetahs may form a *coalition,* a group of two, three, or four members. These are sometimes brothers from the same litter. A coalition makes it easier to hunt large prey like zebra or wildebeest. Female cheetahs hunt alone and therefore often hunt smaller prey.

4
THE HUNTER

A large female cheetah stands on a tall, rocky hill in eastern Africa. She is hungry and thirsty. Her cubs have not eaten in three days. But before hunting, the cheetah must first check to see if there are lions, hyenas, or other cheetahs nearby. Unlike other cats, cheetahs hunt almost entirely during the day. Sharp eyesight and hearing help the mother cheetah to sense whether it is safe to hunt.

The land appears to be clear of other predators. The cheetah spots a herd of Thomson's gazelles, also known as Tommys, about 700 yards (600 m) away. Coming down from the hill and advancing steadily, the cheetah moves along the grasslands. She drops her head and keeps it low and steady, ears pulled back. The cheetah's slim body and spotted coat blend in with the grass.

CHEETAHS HUNT DURING THE DAY. RELYING ON THEIR SHARP EYESIGHT TO HUNT, THEY MAY CLIMB TO A HIGH PLACE TO LOOK FOR PREY AND FOR ENEMIES.

A CHEETAH OBSERVES A HERD OF WILDEBEEST.

The chief advantage that a cheetah's prey has is to get a running start. If the cheetah does not catch the gazelle quickly she risks getting tired from the chase, allowing the prey to escape. But the herd is still quietly grazing as the cheetah approaches. The cheetah spots her target, a young calf that has strayed from its mother. When the cheetah is about 200 feet (61 m) from the herd, the Tommys race away. The cheetah extends the front part of her body, leaping forward with the power of her back legs. Her flexible spine extends, acting like a spring. In seconds, she's running at almost full speed. As the calf tries to dodge and escape, the cheetah follows, changing direction by digging into the ground with heavy claws.

The cheetah lunges at the calf's back leg to trip it, then uses its *dew claw* to grab the calf's back flank. As the calf struggles, the cheetah bites down on its neck, clamping the throat shut until the calf has stopped breathing.

A cheetah's eating habits are unique. The cheetah eats its kill quickly, gorging itself on meat until it is full. Then it abandons the kill, even if there is food left. Unlike other wild cats, the cheetah does not save its kill for later or return for another helping. A cheetah will only eat fresh kill that it catches itself. A cheetah can go as long as a

AN AVERAGE CHASE AFTER PREY MAY LAST NO MORE THAN THIRTY SECONDS, COVERING A DISTANCE OF AS MUCH AS 600 YARDS (546 M).

CHEETAHS KILL THEIR PREY BY CLAMPING THE VICTIM'S WINDPIPE SHUT.

week without food and can last for ten days without drinking water. It gets its water supply mostly from the meat it catches.

The cheetah brings its meal over to a grassy, shady area but cannot yet begin to eat. Exhausted from the chase, the cheetah's large chest heaves in and out. Great speed but little endurance leaves the cheetah so tired after the kill that she must rest for as long as half an hour. The cheetah would be defenseless if a predator were to appear now. Lions, hyenas, and other carnivores frequently chase cheetahs from their kill.

Competition with other predators is one reason why there are few cheetahs in the wild. But the biggest threat to their survival is the human threat.

5
CHEETAHS AND US

A century ago, cheetahs were widespread over Africa, Asia, and India. They numbered over a hundred thousand worldwide. Throughout the twentieth century, as land settlement increased in those countries, the cheetah came into conflict with humans. Thousands of cheetahs were shot or speared by farmers who blamed them for killing livestock. Between 1980 and 1991, almost 7,000 cheetahs were shot by ranchers or killed for trophies in Namibia. The cheetah also fell victim to illegal, organized killing called *poaching*. In the 1980s, gangs of poachers in central Africa shot and killed wildlife, including cheetahs. By the 1990s fewer than 10,000 cheetahs remained in the wild. Cheetahs are now extinct in sixteen African countries.

The area where cheetahs now live is very popular with travelers. Thousands of tourists visit Kenya's Masai Mara

A CHEETAH CLIMBS ON A SAFARI TRUCK AT MASAI MARA NATIONAL GAME RESERVE IN KENYA.

game reserve each year. During the day, when the cheetah's daytime hunting habits coincide with tourist visits, it is a common sight to see a tourist bus or jeep close in on a cheetah and her family. All this attention can interrupt the mother's hunting habits, keeping her from caring for her cubs as she normally would. Although tour operators can be fined for breaking park rules, tour guides will often allow tourists to get very close to a cheetah in order to photograph the cat.

Organized hunting by humans leaves less prey for cheetahs to eat. Cheetahs have also been pushed out of protected game reserves where they compete with other large predators like lions and hyenas. The majority of wild cheetahs live outside of protected game reserves. Today, cheetahs are found mostly in the Serengeti and Mara plains of Tanzania and Kenya, and in Namibia, home to 70 percent of the world's remaining wild cheetah population.

All over the world, scientists are working to save the cheetah from extinction, or disappearing completely. A conservation program based in Namibia trains Anatolian shepherd dogs to protect livestock so ranchers do not have to kill cheetahs that prey on livestock.

OVER ONE HUNDRED ANATOLIAN SHEPHERD DOGS WORK ON FARMS IN NAMIBIA TODAY. THEY GUARD LIVESTOCK AGAINST CHEETAHS.

A MOTHER AND HER CUBS FACE AN UNCERTAIN FUTURE.

Unlike other shepherding dogs, the Anatolian shepherd dog will stand and fight. It also thrives in the dry, hot climate of Africa.

Scientists at zoos have developed a Species Survival Plan (SSP) for cheetahs. This includes a program to breed cheetahs in captivity, choosing male and female cheetahs to mate and produce healthy cubs. But unlike other endangered wild cats, the cheetah has been very difficult to breed in captivity. At first, many cubs born to captive cheetahs died from diseases. But by 1987, North American zoos began to successfully breed cheetahs. The number of healthy cheetahs in zoos has continued to increase. There is hope that these cheetahs and their offspring will eventually be reintroduced into the wild.

Through programs like this one, we can begin to secure the future for the world's fastest land animal.

camouflage: To hide by blending into surroundings.

coalition: A group of two or more adult male cheetahs that live and hunt together.

coursing: An ancient sport in which cheetahs were trained hunters.

den: The place where cheetah cubs are raised.

dew claw: A claw 4 inches (10.3 cm) above the inside claw of an animal's foot.

domestic: An animal that has been bred by humans.

litter: A group of newborn cubs.

mantle: The smoky-gray fur seen on the tops of newborn cheetah cubs' coats.

poaching: Organized illegal hunting.

BOOKS

Barfuss, Matt H. *My Cheetah Family*. Minneapolis, MN: Carolrhoda Books, 1998.

Caro, T.M. *Cheetahs of the Serengeti Plains*. University of Chicago Press, 1994.

Dupot, Phillipe, Valerie Tracqui, and Elena Dworkin Wright. *The Cheetah*. Charlesbridge Publishing, 1992.

Esbesen, Barbara Juster. *Swift as the Wind*. Orchard Books, 1996.

Frame, George and Lory. *Swift and Enduring: Cheetahs and Wild Dogs of the Serengeti*. E.P. Dutton, 1981.

Hunter, Luke. *Cheetahs*. Voyager Press, 2000.

Jensen, C.L. *Cheetahs*. Zoobooks/Wildlife Education, 2000.

MacPherson, Winnie, and John McGee. *Cheetahs for Kids*. NorthWord Press, 1998.

Sullivan, Jody. *Cheetahs: Spotted Speedsters*. Bridgestone Books, 2003.

FICTION

Morrison, Taylor. *Cheetah*. New York: Henry Holt & Company, 1998.

WEBSITES

Cheetah Conservation Fund

www.cheetah.org

National Geographic Kids

www.nationalgeographic.com/kids/creature_feature/0003/cheetah.html

Nature Online

www.pbs.org/wnet/nature/cheetahs/

ABOUT THE AUTHOR

Diana Estigarribia is the author of *Smithsonian National Zoological Park* from the Great Zoos of the United States series. She has also written books on the life sciences, plants, and animal habitats. She is a journalist and researcher for a national magazine and lives in New York with her husband, a novelist and book designer.